Praise for *Brevi...*

"Few writers can turn traditional i[n] ... Loren Niemi. While so many of today's artists surround themselves with noise, Niemi is a Master of silence and negative space. He has been an influencer in the poetry community for years; and, truth be told, I steal from him every chance I get."

> — Danny Klecko, author of *Hitman-Baker-Casket Maker: Aftermath of an American's Clash with Ice*

"Gratitude for Loren Niemi's gift of poetry! He helps us see the beauty in the detritus and the sacred in every moment."

> — Elizabeth Ellis, author of *Every Day a Holiday*

"Loss is paramount in these poems that traverse the canonical hours of the Catholic religious order, entered by a young Loren. Seeking an epiphany, or maybe to escape the Vietnam war, the hormonal anguish of youth grinds against "those cold chapels". When he stopped wearing the robe, things learned included "how to be alone," driving night cab, picking up John Berryman and teaching art. Niemi reflects on what it means to be at the end of life's journey, calling attention to: 'What changed? You? The world?'"

> —Jules Nyquist, author of *Atomic Paradise*,

"*Breviary of the Lost* is superb. The framework itself is worth the read. Loren and I first met over 50 years ago, and I remain thoroughly impressed by him as an artist whether his work shows up in a frame, a story, a poem, or a memoir. In *Breviary for the Lost*, he is at the top of his game."

> —Bill McCarthy, poet, author of *Past Sins* and *Fall Risk*.

A BREVIARY
FOR THE LOST
Poems for the During and After

CALUMET
EDITIONS

Minneapolis

First Edition July 2022
A Breviary for the Lost: Poems for the During and After. Copyright © 2022
by Loren Niemi. All rights reserved.

Printed in the United States of America.
10 9 8 7 6 5 4 3 2 1
ISBN: 978-1-950743-87-2

Cover photo: Diego Vazquez
Back cover photo: Jeff Strate
Cover and book design by Gary Lindberg

A BREVIARY
FOR THE LOST
Poems for the During and After

LOREN NIEMI

**CALUMET
EDITIONS**
Minneapolis

Also by Loren Niemi

Prose

Inviting the Wolf In: Thinking About Difficult Stories
(with Elizabeth Ellis)

The New Book of Plots

Point of View and the Emotional Arc of Stories
(with Nancy Donoval)

What Haunts Us

Poetry

Coyote Flies Coach

Vote Coyote!

For David, Donald, Gregory and K. Basil who have passed through the veil but remain close to my heart and all those religious, storytellers, artists, and poets, then and now, who made my lived community possible.

Author's Note

I began writing poems to capture moments of what I considered an ordinary life, and over the course of fifty plus years they have become evidence of just how unordinary my life has been. This collection focuses on my years in the Christian Brothers, a Catholic religious teaching order, and the echo of that experience afterwards.

Matins

Before I Entered

Brother Bruno came to see my parents
And while they sat in the living room
Discussing what becoming a religious [1]
Would mean, I sat in the basement
At the drum kit left over from last night's
Party tapping out a 4/4 shuffle
And though I was unconscious of it,
It was my way of saying that I too
Was a part of their conversation
Even if I was not in the room.

What Bruno said to them or they to him
Was never said to me, though
My father did say that I'd be getting
A better education than he could afford.
What I did not say then, could not say,
Would not say until many years later
Was that it was the only sure way
I knew to avoid Vietnam which
In '65 might have seemed alarmist
But by '69 would be prophetic.

[1]
When he is asked why he joined
A Catholic religious order –
His answers are often glib,
The truth complicated.

He was not
Particularly religious though
He had been an altar boy
But even that was more about
The theater of it:
The candles, incense,
The mystery of mumbled Latin
That meant little
Even when he understood it.

In the traditional literature
They talk about being "called"
To a vocation and he was
Though if he had known
It would be to a life after
Poverty, Chastity and Obedience,
After the years of trying,
Only to be tossed out,
He might have rejected the call

Another Time, Another Place

My body learned the Novitiate clock: [2]
The sameness of days a second heartbeat
A constant until the moment it falters.

5:30 - Rising from the narrow bed for chapel chill
6:30 – The celebration of Catholic mass and
       Summer light piercing the stained glass
7:30 – Cornbread, runny scrambled eggs,
       Coffee in silence

8:00 – I was once told the "work is practice for habit
       Not perfection" and so it was
9:00 – Interrupted for a Breviary's marking of hours
9:30 – Theology seemed to me as architecture
       Is to building, formal but not necessarily
       A house you can live in
11:30 - Interrupted to pray again
12:00 - Bread, soup, milk or water, never wine

1:00 – It is manual labor on even days,
       Team sports on odd
4:30 – An hour to call your own to read,
       Sometimes sneak a smoke

5:30 – Praying again I measured the fading light
6:00 - Meat and potatoes, bread without butter,
       Sometimes a little sweet dessert

6:30 - The walk to the highway and back
       Becomes my true meditation.
7:00 - Study, I was told, read, consider but

[2]
Like the army, the novitiate
Was formative,
A shock to the system
Driven by rules and schedule
Designed to make him,
Not in God's image and likeness,
For he was already endowed
With those attributes –
God creates, God Blesses,
God chastises
For the sake of Justice,
God forgives – but instead
To mold him in
A tradition of discipline
And assumed piety.

He accepted
What he could and
Found ways around the rest.

More often I went downstairs [3}
To shoot a little 8-ball.
9:00 – On Friday "advertisements" also know
    As "the correction of faults"
9:30 – I'd pray the Breviary's last hour, Compline
    And those words:
    "Your enemy as a roaring lion, seeks
    Someone to devour, resist him...."
10:00 – A nightly silence follows that of the day.

Out the window the college across the valley
Twinkled in the dark, an invitation
To the life I had left –

To walk there would be simple enough,
A fateful choosing, another time, another place,
Once made would not be walked back.

[3]
The soundtrack
Of his formative life was
Bifurcated:
"Your blessing Lord,
Bestow unto us…"
Of Gregorian chants
On one side and
The Animals,
"We gotta get
Out of this place, if it's the
Last thing we ever do,"
On the other.

Walking to the Highway

After we had all the silence
We could choke down
With the meat and potatoes,
After the stacking of the dishes
The uncomplaining Mexican nuns [4]
Would wash, we would walk to the highway -
Down the hill and across a bridge -
A full mile to the road and another back.

I don't know where he got them
But one night Marty J. had cigarettes
Handed out for any taker and
Joyfully lit when we were out of sight.
A savored sharing while we joked
Like the teens we actually were instead
Of whomever we were supposed to be
After taking vows and robes.

Summer heat, winter cold, it made
No difference whether it is light
Or dark, tramping with or without gloves
And coat, I welcomed the ritual
Thinking more than once that
When I got to the road I'd stick out
My thumb and climb into the first
18-wheeler that stopped.

Thinking is not doing.
Crush the butt underfoot and turn
Back on the gravel path, over the bridge,
Up the hill deaf to complaints voiced
Under far dim stars, imagining

[4]
In high school he had two
Girlfriends, the one at the
Catholic school his sister
Went to, who worked
At a grocery store
On Saturday nights
And the one who went to
Public school he only saw
On Saturday nights.

He asked himself why he
Hadn't slept with either
Before taking vows
But a contrarian thought
Was - how could you miss
What you never had?

What he had was a hand
And an imagination that left
Stains on the sheets.

One night he considered
The Mexican nuns who did
The laundry – did they
Count how many sheets
Held unwanted seed?

Tomorrow would be different;
That it would be the day I would pack,
Or find a reason to stay.

They never walked
To the highway
But lived a life that was
An indentured servitude
Of prayer, cooking, laundry
And he wondered was it enough?
Did they also dream
What another life could offer?

Brother John Watching Bergman

For reasons that were unexplained
But appreciated by me at least,
Brother John, the Novitiate Director [5]
Had a love of films, especially foreign
Films, and every month we would
Watch something with subtitles.

Bergman's "7th Seal", "Wild Strawberries",
"Through a Glass Darkly" and then
Fellini's "8½", "La Dolce Vita", "La Strada",
Or Truffaut's "400 Blows", even "Jules
And Jim" though it could not compare
To "The Seven Samurai" or "Throne of Blood".

There might've been theology in his intent
But I was thinking not about my spirituality
Or God's mercy when chapel prayer failed
To keep me awake. Those flickering screens
Were my moral education – a vocabulary
Worth keeping – a celluloid gospel in B&W.

[5]
The Rule was unraveling.

Whether Brother Director
John saw the future or
Simply gave up on the past
Was yet to be determined.

He did not notice the slipping
Away as much as the
Additions – the appearance
Of Commonweal magazine and
The Catholic Worker
In the common room,
A Joan Baez album played
Instead of Bartok one night –
All offered without comment.

He dared not comment,
Least these glimpses of
Culture beyond the valley
Would go missing,
Once more shrouded
In don't and can't.

Thanksgiving

Perhaps it was to take our minds off
The family tables we were not going
To sit at or perhaps it was just to work up

An appetite, the announcement came.
We were going to take a 5-mile hike
And dutifully climbed on the back

Of the flatbed. Brother John drove
Us out of the valley, up county road 21
Until there was nothing but farm fields and

Wooded crevices partially obscured
By snow where streams flowed beneath
A widening shroud of gray November ice.

We tumbled out and sorted ourselves
Into those who were quick as if arriving
Back at the Novitiate would feed any

Of us before those who hung
Back to smoke cigarettes and tell stories
Of life before taking the robe finally arrived.

Walk we did down the gravel road to
The paved until we arrived at the turn
Onto the gravel road the led to our nod

To tradition – turkey, mashed potatoes,
Gravy, peas, yeast rolls and pumpkin pie –
All a bit drier than I would have liked,

Eaten in silence while we Brothers
Took turns reading the account of Jesus [6]
Feeding the multitude loaves and fishes.

[6]
From his room he could see
The lights of the college
Beyond the dividing ravine
Where a little stream ran
Between dark banks.

Over there, a library with books,
Magazines, a reminder
of the world, he was supposed
To have renounced.

Over here, the texts
Proscribed for safety and edification
Read at meals or study sessions.

Neither the Bible nor prayer book
Kept him from thinking
He might cross that stream,
Climb the hill, slip unnoticed
Into the student union,
Not for a soda, but to get
Any newspaper that would tell him
The names of the war dead
Or which politician was caught
With which mistress.

My Prayer

I prayed
And prayed again
Hoping to still
My hunger for faith or
Even a better doubt.   [7]

Like communion wafers
Stuck to the roof
Of your mouth,
My belief now dry
On the tongue,

Choked when not
Chewed and still…
In grade school I had wanted
To be a holy one, blessed,
A saint, whose good work

Shines forth,
Whose miracles are
Not matters of dispute.
Did I hope to hear angel
Wings brush the pew?

Now I am wondering
How long, Jesus,
Will I have
To wait in silence
Before finally letting go

[7]
He was not sure that any
Prayers would be answered
In spite of the repetition
Of ritual hours. The open
Breviary's matins, lauds, and
The rest – every brittle page
Of the small book inside a leather
Zippered cover - seemed
An anarchism, as foreign as the
Latin text which appeared on
The left.

The lesson he took from it
Was not solace but
A kind of accommodation
That would appear over and over,
Substituting something familiar
But irrelevant
For asking a question that might
Require you to confront an
Uncomfortable answer.

Of this calcified theology?
Shall my lived days
Determine the outcome
And welcome my
Nascent agnosticism? Amen.

The Coats

In the basement, mysteries   [8]
And treasures were found
On dusty storeroom shelves.

Along one wall bins with black
Cotton or twill pants (some well-worn,
Others new or almost new) neatly
Folded in stacks with no discernable
Sizing next to boxes of heavy knit
Sweaters, all navy blue or black.

Other shelves held what we called
Bunny boots - Army surplus gear with
Hard rubber shells and fleece linings.

In the center of the room
Three rows of piping with robes
And coats hanging with short on
One end and long on the other.

I had no interest in the robes as
I had two, one to wear, one to spare,
But the coats, they called out --
Come try a warm Navy pea or a dashing
Kaki trench coat. I wondered if
I put one on would I feel the vibration
Of the life that had once wore it?

The shape of shoulders, the tear
At the elbow, the story of the missing
Button and once, a pipe left
In a pocket. It was a good pipe,

[8]
The great mystery
First, last and always
Was what was not said.
Except in a kind of code,
Short hand of another era,
A misdirected, warning about
"Particular friendships"
The primary example.

In this century of outing
Pedophile priests it is hard
To remember
The great silence that
Made it possible.

"It" being desire – unfulfilled,
Sublimated, not acted on –
Though those attracted to
One's own had more
Opportunity than those
Attracted to difference.
As one attracted to difference
He did not see
How particular some
Friendships were.

And if he had, what difference
Would it have made?

With a short of stem and a walnut
Bowl blackened by familiarity. I carefully
Put it back in the same pocket.

I'd slip in at the end of the day
Just to smell the sweat of other lives
And hold that pipe, trying to imagine
Who and what, when, and where
It had been before it arrived at this
Pause in a Novitiate storeroom.

He would come to believe
That was how you found your way
Through communal life -
A wink, a nod,
Booze, golf or the gym,
As long as you were
Discrete, the unspoken
Permission would be offered.

Lauds

Poem for the Epiphany

In dreams
The answers came
To follow stars,
To not trust authority,
To leave for Egypt
Before the slaughter
Of innocents.

It was never about
The gold, frankincense
Or myrrh but always
About the journey
Directed by dreams,
A pressing answer to
An unasked question.   [9]

I was, as they were,
Open to warnings dreamt
Though in my case
It was to stay,
Believing change
Was coming
To those cold chapels.

[9]
In summer they would
Rip rap the stream
Beneath the bridge.
In fall, after bulldozers
Finished rearranging
The valley narrows, he
Rip rapped the earthen
Dam conservation
Funds had paid for.

There was a tempo
To hauling and heaving
Stones that left him
Walking that weighted gait
The rest of the day,
And when the bed
Was at last claimed, He would feel the slow
Unclenching and welcome
A dreaming that was not
The stone's measure of progress.

He does not remember what
They did in winter –
Strip old wax, reseal floors,
Paint walls another shade
Of unobtrusive white or
The kind of green that should
Be reserved for ice cream –
Seemed probable.

Signs of Liberalization

1.
After the Novitiate year
We marched with our suitcases
Down the road, across the bridge
That separated the centuries,
Up the hill to the Scholasticate
For our delayed college education
Where we were greeted with the words,
"It's better here," and I thought,
"We'll see about that." [10]

2.
We settled in rooms with older
Roommates, in my case, Brother
Vincent, a former navy guy who seemed
To sleep all day and sit by the window

Keeping watch all hours of the night,
And Brother Fabian who lived for
Racketball sweat, basketball sweat,
Baseball sweat, any sweat.

When the first weekend arrived
Vincent said there was beer, as much as
You wanted to drink, so I had one
And then another but what was

The point? Getting drunk had no appeal,
Throwing up had no appeal.
I decided there and then that beer,
Even free beer, wasn't worth having a third.

[10]
The Scholasticate was three
Stories arranged as a U with
The garage and shops
On one end of the first floor,
The library and visitor
Parlors, Brother Director's
Office in the center and
The chapel and common room
At the other end.

Downstairs: the kitchen,
Dining room and a succession
Of storage rooms along a hall
Where whatever entered
Never came out.

Above the garage were
Basketball and handball
Courts with Brothers rooms
Filling the remainder of
The 2nd and 3rd floors,

3.
When we stopped wearing the robe
It went into the closet and I took
On my generation's uniform, the one
I actually wore until graduation.

Blue jeans, often with cowboy boots,
A white shirt most of the time,
But when ceremony warranted,
Which was often enough, I'd add

A vest, of which I had two – a small gray
Herringbone for everyday and a butternut
Tan suede for formalities except the once
A year that brought the robe out of the closet.

4.
In my senior year for an advanced painting [11]
Class I took a cue from Claes Oldenberg,
Giving my old jeans six coats of white enamel
And mounting them on a red base.

It hung in the hall next to a water fountain.
Ten years later when visiting old haunts
It was still there, though the frame
Had warped so badly it seemed

To be stepping away from the wall.
I considered remounting it but thought
If I could leave, surely it could also
Depart any time it wanted to.

Though a barbershop was
Tucked into what should have
Been a closet on the 2nd floor.

[11]
He found a way to balance
Study for the expected degree in
Religious Studies (which really
Was Philosophy though
The Order did not like calling it that)
And a major in Studio Arts
Where he took classes at the other
Catholic College in town.

He commandeered a room with windows
In the shop wing and made it
His studio. Mostly he made paintings,
Political silk screens, but sometimes
Sculptures, when required.
If you wanted to talk
That was the place to find him.
If you wanted a cup of coffee,
You had to bring it with you.

For Michael P.

In the Scholasticate, '67 was
The year of the exodus; when the
Common room started with desks
Cheek to jowl and as they left,
You and I or Tommy K, would haul

The departed's desk out to storage,
To a graveyard really. Whatever was
In the drawers stayed in the drawers. We
Never opened them and why should we?
The next day or two, there would

Be another one to take away until finally
There were so few desks left in the
Big room that no one would study
In the land of ghosts. It was a hard
Year that one, with the two of us [12]

In the end room on the 2nd floor
Where you cried out in French in your
Dreaming. I didn't know French
But if I didn't answer you something
You'd bolt upright, wanting to know

What was that, where were we and
Who was at the door? Was it those who
Thought the Church was going to Hell
In a hand basket or those boys who wanted
You to come out to play let's pretend

[12[
Change was going to come
And did, though
Vatican II was largely cosmetic.
Even with a new set and lyrics
For the old musical,
The starring roles had
The same solemn men in front,
The dutiful nuns behind.

In a "Kumbaya" moment
The table was turned,
English was as plain spoke
As the newly revised liturgy,
The bread got chewy,
The music got groovy,
Or what passed for it
With two guitars and
Michael P. playing the bass.

In the moonlit orchard or just me trying
To get back into the room after a night
Drinking with Jennie O. who dug politics
As much as Mingus, she of Black Russians
The way Jimmy the bartender made them. [13]

I didn't know how good I had it with you
Caught between faith and unrequited love
Until years later when I would wake with
A girlfriend's bad dream ringing in my ears
I'd think of you, *a bien dormi*

[13]
He drank in two town bars.

Charlie's D&B was
A smoky "scar bar" in every sense
Of the word that still managed
To be neutral ground
With a decent jukebox
And enough selection to
Satisfy both bikers and hippies.

The Four Queens was
Mostly dark, the kind of place
You went to sit unnoticed
At a small table in the back
While in front, bartender
Jimmy mixed classic
Cocktails with a minimum
Of conversation behind a
Horseshoe bar with statues
Of Greek Goddesses at each end.

Reading D.H. Lawrence

At the end of the hall, I found him
Hidden in a closet, with the others
We were not supposed to read, at
Least "not yet", whatever the Hell
That meant. Who put them there,
Whether Brother Director trying to keep
Us safe, or some Devil knowing the value
Of temptation did not matter. I knew they
Were there and because they were there
I would wrest their meaning from the dust.

Sons and Lovers which I thought was [14]
Awkward (such a naive judgment) followed
By *Women in Love*, then *The Man Who Died*
Which burned into my imagination
With such ferocity that I could stroke
My still virgin cock to attention with
The images of Jesus and Mary Magdalene
Therein. If this was sin, I was a sinner.

[14]
D.H. Lawrence led to
Gunther Grass' *The Tin Drum* led to
Samuel Beckett's *Waiting for Godot*
And once it was in his hands
He knew he had found the measure
Of his condition in that text.

As Vladimir says "Let us do something,
while we have the chance! It is not every
day that we are needed. Not indeed that
we personally are needed. Others would
meet the case equally well, if not better.
To all mankind they were addressed,
those cries for help still ringing in our ears!
But at this place, at this moment of time,
all mankind is us, whether we like it or not.
Let us make the most of it, before it it too late!"

Meeting Barbara

I thank SDS or more specifically a young
Tom Hayden for inviting a few of us
Who were at the anti-war convocation
Back to his motel room to drink a little
Whiskey from paper cups and talk of

Organizing the Revolution. There the girl
From Duluth with the dark eyes told me
That she went to my mother's alma
Mater, and was in fact, in the nursing
Program as was my mother years before.

The night wore on, a flirtation commenced [15]
Till gray morning when we left arm in arm
Not quite drunk but certainly not sober
To have what would be the first picture
Of us taken for my FBI file.

.

[15]
The joke he tells is that he was
A member of a religious
Order with vows of
Poverty, Chastity and
Obedience. He was good at
One of them.

When he is asked about
The sex thing there
Is not much, or rather,
Too much to say…

At 21 he was still a virgin.
At 22 he was not.
It was unplanned.

It happened on a couch
Fueled by red wine and
Grief watching the Chicago
Democratic convention
With the sound of police sirens
And breaking glass as
The soundtrack.

He loved her but not enough
To leave the Order.
She loved him but not
Enough to tell him that
She was an FBI informant,
Or so he surmised

Looking at the facts
After the fact,
After she disappeared.

It was a sign of the times.

Summer on Nicollet Island

Trout Mask Replica is blasting on the stereo,
As I'm doing the last joint Doug Wood
Gave me before I head out the door
To start driving cab with the windows
Rolled down in still summer heat.

Downstairs the Brothers are playing
Gin Rummy, Bridge, or maybe Go Fish,
Anything to pass the time between
The ice in this glass of cheap whiskey
And the next one. The baseball game is
On as Brother Richard asks me to sit in.

Can't do it, not because I dislike cards,
Or that I don't care to interact,
But their time is not mine;
I'm driving cab midnight to 9 AM and
After that heading over to the art factory
To get my printmaking class work done
Before the heat is thicker than the ink.

Last night the other Brother Giles stumbled
In bloody and bruised telling me
He'd been robbed on a walk but what
Did he expect stopping in the Gay '90's
For a quick one? I could've told him it
Was dangerous to troll rough trade.

Makes no difference what he's into --
To each their own. When it comes to
Stumbling under the yoke of celibacy

I glossed over most older Brothers drinking
Themselves to a functional numbness.

The night of the Apollo moon landing
I did sit with them to raise a glass
As the grainy image of a man making
A small step flickered on the screen.

When it was done, I went down to [16]
The river, delivered the news and some
Cigarettes to the old hobos camping there.
They raised their paper bags in salute
To the moon, then drank as they do;
Stared at the smoky fire, shrugged
And went back to broken lives
Held as close as the freedom they claimed.

I went to my transient's bed, back to
The question I turned like a nervous coin --
What would I claim as my "small step"
Before I could depart for terra incognita?

[16]
Minneapolis was a different
City then, rougher around the edges
with the so-called urban renewal
Of the Gateway District and construction
Of the freeway driving the poor towards
Neighborhoods that would
Soon be subject to another displacement.

On Nicollet Island
Hennepin Avenue was fronted on each
Side with three and four-story brick buildings –
Island Bicycle, Mitch's Liquor, Angstrom Shoes –
With rooms above that alcoholics and railroad
Workers could afford by the night or week.

North of Hennepin was De La Salle,
The Catholic high school the Brothers ran.
He stayed there while taking University classes.

Behind De La Salle - an auto repair shop,
A limestone rooming house, the railroad tracks
Bisecting the island, then run-down houses
Sheltering old Beats, young Hippies,
Innumerable dogs, a wandering donkey.

At the northern most tip of the island, the guys
Who rode the freights and didn't want or couldn't
Afford a flop house bed, would sit around a fire
Talking about everything except how they came
To be drinking from a paper bag.

Driving Cab

Leaving De La Salle, I cross the parking lot,
The Hennepin Avenue bridge.
Slide into the Yellow cab garage to punch in,
Grab a working rig [17]
With at least a half full tank,
Roll down the window in the summer heat
And spend the better part of the night
Ferrying drunks
From twilight barstool
To flop house,
To after-hours joint,
To some approximation of home
And the waiting wife, or no wife at all.

I picked up John Berryman at the Copper Squirrel,
Dropped him off in Prospect Park once,
Never bothered to say
I really like your poetry or the class at the U
I sat in on 'cause in no mood for small talk
The poet nodded off most of the way.
No, the only thing I did say was,
"Hey, buddy, what was that address again?"

At 1 AM it's closing time,
The bar rush to get somewhere, anywhere,
Because by 3 AM
The end of the party rolls around,
At 4 AM the vampires look for their crypt,
From 5 and 6 AM it's early workers,
The ones who make the office and factories hum
Before the guys with ties arrive,

[17]
Night after night he drove
Until which streets were fastest,
Why the airport was to be
Avoided after 10 PM,
Which calls to which bars
Would provide decent tips,
Were embedded as habit.

The voice of the dispatcher
Part drill sergeant,
Part jokester and sometimes
A little of soothing mother,
Crackled over the radio,
Disembodied,
Keeping vigil with him.

The night changed by the hours,
Deepening to bruised black
As lights turned out,
Then to the still dark of moonlight,
Followed by creeping of 5 AM
Purple becoming rose before
The sun's red crown appeared
Between office towers.

The one time he agreed to do a
Day shift, the second ticket

Followed at 7 AM by business travelers
Heading to the airport for the early flights
And by 9 AM I'm punching out
$40 cash tipped bucks
For nine hours in my pocket.

Pulled a gun, robbed him
Of the $20 chump change starter.
That day the dispatcher had
No sympathy, the cops had
No interest, and he still had eight
Hours to try to make the day pay.

Prime

Meeting Jennie

The way I tell it there was a benefit
For draft resistance with a BBC documentary
About Bob, a local guy who burned his cards
And went to prison for conscience.

There was a scene where his fiancé
Ran through a field of flowers a la
Elvira Madigan. Soft focus. Slow motion.
I watched her enlarged braless breasts

Rise and fall on screen, thinking
That must hurt and when the lights came
On, there she was, standing in front of me.
It was all I could do to not ask, [18]

If she was wearing a bra but the answer
Would come on the day we chained
Ourselves to the cathedral communion rail
To protest the Bishop's support of the war.

[18]
Little did he know that after 50 years
He could still see the girl who flirted
With him in the back yard of student
Ghetto housing.

It was summer session on the East Bank,
Fans struggled to move heat but the smell
Of the French fry factory, the smell of her
Suntan lotion dominated the afternoon.

He was reading a script – *A Taste of
Honey* – as she cut his hair, her
Generous breasts brushing against his
Bare back.

How could he not have a hard on?
Too embarrassed to turn and take her
In his arms, to kiss her or bed her there
On the fresh watered lawn
He thought about that afternoon
for months. Unsure of what she had
Wanted, he was afraid that he would
Have disappointed the both of them.

If their lives were measured by
Postponements
Of every could have been,
They made the most of what they chose.

The Revolution Comes

1.
After we removed the furniture
From the little room across from the library
We painted the walls black,
Brought in a bunch of cushions
Watched the Smothers Brothers
On someone's old B&W television.

2.
Someone decided that the old communion
Wafers were too likely to get stuck
On the roof of your mouth
And replaced them with real bread,
A thick sourdough you had to chew thoroughly
If you didn't want Jesus to choke you.

3.
Kathy K. came on Sunday, Jennie O. too. [19]
First for the Post-Vatican II mass and then
Dinner with roast beef and potatoes the Mexican
Nuns cooked. Afterwards they would flirt with
The cute, smart, often red-faced Brothers with
Hard-ons beneath their black robes.

4.
When Brother Director Gregory sent me
To Chicago to study Protestant Theology
He did not know that it would come with
A heaping helping of Saul Alinsky or that
I would return an anti-war and anti-draft organizer
Who could quote Paul Tillich at the teach-in.

[19]
To his mind it was
Natural that they would
Welcome the smart,
Politically liberal if not
Radical, and yes, "easy
On the eyes" (as
They used to say) women
Into the community.

It also seemed
Natural that Brothers
Or nuns would leave
For love and marriage.
When John S. left it
Was to marry Kathy K.

He didn't leave,
Though if pressed
He would admit
That he had a crush
On Jennie O.
But whether he loved
Her for herself or
The fact that she was
A dedicated anti-war
Organizer
Did not matter. She was
There and he was glad she was.

5.
Sunshine Superman was playing on the radio
Before the news told us Bobby Kennedy was dead.
I could not hear birds singing June songs though
It was still a warm summer's day until Pat M said,
"That's it, I'm done, I'm leaving..." and turned up
The volume for the Stones' *Jumping Jack Flash*.

6.
In the library I find a notebook without name and
Written within: "It is not the sacred books that count
Or sacraments with their oils and priestly unction.
My community is a secret society of Poets, Philosophers,
Mystics, and unnamed Saints who recognize each other
By our contrary works, done of necessity or joy." [20]

[20]
He recognized the community
He called his own were not
The members of the Order
In safe suburban schools but
The blue denim activists marching
In the street and the artists sharing
Portuguese wine as they argued
Whether Warhol was passe or Fellini
Would ever make another movie
As good as *La Dolce Vita*.

The division was not limited to
The Scholasticate, the college, the town
But the whole of America. Liberal
Or conservative, for or against the war,
Civil Rights, Women's rights, whatever
The subject the fault lines were manifest
And there was little room for nuance.

Marching for Futility

We were small in number -
A few dozen or so students from
The three colleges – St. Mary's,
St. Theresa's. and Winona State,
Marching down Main Street
To "End the war" with a squad
Car in front and another behind.

The reporter from the local   [21]
Paper walked a block or two
Shouting the usual questions
As the guys from the Marine
Fraternity, Semper Fi,
Called us "fags" and "Commies"
And threw empty beer cans.

Five blocks seemed enough to
Make the point that not
Everyone was in favor of "bombing
Them back to the Stone Age" when
We split into two factions –
Those who went back to the start,
Those who stepped into the bar.

When the Semper Fi guys arrived
At Charlie's D&B they skipped the easy
Insults and ordered beers. same as us.
I wanted to tell them, before fists flew,
We are not opposed to the flag,
Apple pie or motherhood, just
Your dying for profit and politics.

[21]
He did the usual things you did
In those days: attend peace marches,
Or sit at tables handing out
Anti-draft pamphlets,
Or speak at teach-ins while
Liberal faculty wearing turtle-necks
Flirted with undergrad girls.

He did some things that were not usual
Like driving to another
City to meet with other organizers,
Drinking in cheap motel rooms
As they planned other, bigger demonstrations
While the FBI sat in obvious cars taking
Photos of those entering or leaving.

After a while he knew all the activists
In Winona, some of those
In Minneapolis or Milwaukee but
For the life of him, no one in Chicago.

History would say that his involvement
Was "marginal" and that was fine with him.
It was not about headlines but about getting
Another voter to the polls to support a different politics.

K. Basil in the News

The newspaper article said
That Catholic "radicals" had
Taken 5000 files from a draft
Board in Milwaukee, burned
Them with homemade napalm
Then stood praying as they
Waited for arrest and so it was
Complete with blurry photograph.

I recognized some of the names,
Brother K. Basil O'Leary's most
Of all – he was a Marxist Economics
Professor at the same college
I attended, a member of
The religious order I claimed,
The man who taught me the value
Of drinking a good single malt.

He was not the first Brother to
Burn draft files. That was
Brother David Darst, another in
The service of the poor I claimed.
He did his burning in Catonsville, MD
With the better known, Dan and Phillip
Berrigan, and was now awaiting
His own government prosecution.

These are facts but the facts do
Not speak what I felt – that I
Should have been on the train
That took K. Basil to Milwaukee to
Test my courage or prove my belief

But on that day, I sat at a table
In the Student Center telling
Whoever would listen: resist. [22]

Same difference you say, individual
Or collective, but wearing the robe
I am not at risk and some said it was
Hypocrisy to tell those who are,
Do this for yourself, for your friends,
And for the sake of peace and justice,
For your country which is ass deep
In a quagmire and sinking fast.

[22]
'Nam was always as close
As Walter Cronkite or Time,
Life, the dammed
Winona Daily News which
Was all for dropping "The big one"
And having a religious
Exemption made his politics
Fierce or false depending
On your own proclivities.

One gift of being a
Brother was he had time
And to a surprising degree,
The freedom to engage in
That anti-war and anti-draft
Organizing.

A teach-in? Yes.
Student strike? Yes.
Occupy the Cathedral? Yes.
Have the FBI ask
The Registrar's office
To see his records? Yes.
Drive to St Louis
To see David Darst before
And after Catonsville? Yes.
Write a paper for
K. Basil's last Philosophy
Symposium that got
Him kicked out of the
Education Department? Yes.

Drive to Milwaukee
For K. Basil's arraignment,
And later, the trial? Yes.
Visit Basil serving
Two years in the Whales
Correctional facility? Yes.

He would not let himself
Be exempt from
The war at home.

May 1970

On a day like this or
That bruised May morning [23]
I was hung over after
My college graduation when
The bikers from down at Charlie's
Bar parked full bore Harley's
On the front porch, drank moonshine
From paper cups, congratulated me.

Mad Donald was still alive,
Still a Brother, still gay,
Still closeted but not so much
So that he did not
Blow one of those leather boys
Or be blown by the girl that loved
Him but did not know, or pretended
Not to know, what was what.

Blessed Brother Giles was still alive,
Still a Brother, still dropping acid
Like it was Aspirin,
Too far gone to be hung over
For another three days
And after two night's tripping
Not the man I wanted making
Eggs in what was left of the kitchen.

David was dead and K. Basil
Was finishing the first of his prison years
For burning draft files. The war raged on.

[23]
Senior year he
Left the Scholsticate for
A little rented gray house
In town on Huff Street,
Across from Winona State
And an easy walk home
From the Four Queens.

Donald, Giles S. and himself
Were the nucleus
With Big Jim and Terry
Of the one testicle
There sometimes but
Not always.

There was no girlfriend
Platonic or otherwise
That year to listen to
Simon & Garfunkel or
CSNY for a mellow or
Captain Beefheart and the
Magic Band or MC5 for
That harsher edge.

Baba Ram Das had said
"Be here now" and they were.

If it was frat house
It was tiny.
If it was a religious community
It was expansive.

Yes, it raged on, with bloody Kent State
Still in the news as I looked
To my future as a wrong man
In the wrong place at the right time
Drinking the last of the orange juice.

Hiking with Earl

After waiting out the thunderstorm
We walked the river's South Branch
Between greening curtains of aspen
And a rainbow rising from the far end
Of the misted valley. [24]

He stopped talking of artists now dead -
Of the brushes they made and the arsenic
In the handmade colors killing them as sure
As syphilis and booze – yet their creations
Are evidence of God's hand in this world.

Rabbits took zigzag courses
While he fiddled for the tobacco
Pouch in his pocket, then
The familiar motions of filling
Cherry wood bowl once more.

We pause. Earl strikes a kitchen
Match on his parka's zipper
Lights up, exhales, puffs again
As a breeze catches the small cloud,
Lifting the incense of satisfaction.

Earl points with pipe in hand
To the red fox watching us.
His color is that of old sumac.
Three quick steps take him
Into the gone of shadowed brush.

[24]
He graduated and was offered
(Or was assigned) a position
Teaching Art in Appleton, WI.

Brother Director Gregory took
Him aside to tell him that the days
Of his "liberation" were over, he would
Have to give up experimenting with
Whatever he was smoking, drinking
Or who knows what else they did
In the house on Huff St.
And come back to the Scholasticate.

He said it was just for the summer.
A necessary step before professional life
In the community of teaching Brothers.

His solace was the frequent walks
He took with Earl Potvin, who had been
Both teacher and mentor for his art major.
Larger than life, Earl demonstrated
A robust engagement with the world.

In the back of his mind, when Earl asked
What he was committed to beyond
Making Art, he blurted out that he had
Entered the Order as a so-so Catholic

Earl says, "here ends today's lesson -
Nature provides if we would but see."
Then turns back towards the car
Parked next to a farm silo,
Five miles that a way.

And after five years of serious religious study
(Mixed with Catholic Worker social activism)
He was leaving Winona
As a bad Buddhist at best and at worst,
A fallen away Unitarian or philosophical
Agnostic, if you wanted to split hairs.

Mad Donald at the Wheel

These highways we travel
Should be called Purgatory,
A dream of two-lane blacktop
Suspended between solitude and
Those who serve, the ones who
Make truck stop coffee taste like wine
Or would release the menageries of
Mangy bobcats and rabbits
With deer antlers strapped to their heads
Populating small town gas stations.

We did not know how rare those stops
Were in the lifetime of delays,
Detours, accidents we found
Or found us when every blind turn
Could be called Dead Man's Curve.

When we heard the news careening
Through the Kentucky Hills
Of four dead at Kent State
You drove with your eyes shut,
Your tears a waterfall.
Some gas station jockey said
It served them right but
What did he know?
Nothing he offered would heal
A heart yearning for justice.

We learned lasting lessons [25]
Early, learned them well,
Wrote them on broken bones
For the sake of a working man's children,
For the love of street corner prophets.

Holy the driving, you said,
Holy the turning wheel,
Holy the coffee cup good to the last drop,
Holy the empty bottle,
Holy the night,
Holy the last toke of whatever was
     Rolled in that yellowed paper
     We found in the glove compartment,
Holy the dawn blessed by
The 18-wheelers clearing a path for us.

[25]
In the twenty-seven years
Between Donald arriving
At the Scholasticate door
Till the scattering of his ashes
In a January rose garden,
They drove someplace,
And whatever detours
That came with it,
At least once every year.

Donald was a great companion
But a terrible driver,
Prone to distraction and
Theological digression.
He missed turns, failed to merge
While espousing as a rule:
Feast one day and fast the next.

Accused of emulating *On the Road*
He was not Kerouac's Sal Paradise.
Donald was not Dean Moriarty
Though Donald might have considered
It a compliment at the time.

Terce

Teaching

I am dedicated to the proposition that:
   Students deserve respect
As responsible and changing persons
To share as much time and friendship
    As you are willing to return
In the misadventure we call making art.

When you create you'll find that you've crossed
   A threshold between the known
And the "accident" of form,
Color, image - between the moment
    You did not see or hear
Or say or feel "X" and the moment you do...

The act of making shifts the world
   Even if it is something as
Pedestrian as eating of a bowl of oatmeal.

Let us praise oatmeal! [26]

I am dedicated to the proposition that:
   Art cannot be taught.
What can be taught is technique.
What can be talked about is theory.
   What can be studied is history.
What can be played with is imagination.

I am not a cop. Not your parent.
   Maybe not even your teacher.
I am not a lot of things you (or I) might wish me to be

[26]
He enjoyed teaching Art
in a Fox Valley Catholic high school.

Even if it was an uneasy fit
with parents and other faculty
Looking at him as little more then
A "hippie" in a corduroy sport coat.
At least for some students,
He was a lifeline out of a conservative
Culture that had spawned
Senator Joe McCarthy.

Or ought to be by dint of rote and role.
Do not trust those expectations.
I am a human being, trying to make our learning enjoyable.

So, pick up your tools and plunge into it as if the journey
Through the sometimes bewildering
Landscape of possibility, is a journey of true discovery.

Let us praise the unknown and bless the travelling!!!

In fact, Joe McCarthy's final resting place
Was a few blocks away.
Years later, he blamed himself for
What became of Greta Van Susteren
(At Fox News,) as once on a field trip
She stepped on Old Joe's grave.
He was sure Old Joe's spirit
Found a welcome as he entered her.

At the end of the year,
When he got a call asking if
He wanted to work in a pilot program
For Juvenile Justice offenders.
He took the offer.

My Classroom

There are day glow psychedelic posters and
Spiderman comic illustrations on the wall.

A record player serves up as much
Blues and jazz as I can get away with.

My classroom is a "check yourself in" room
With art project guides and grades to choose from.

Students might be late but they all came
And every few weeks I'd notice

There were students in the room who were
Not in the grading book but there for the safety

Of a teacher who was not going to send you
To the Principal's office for the joke you told. [27]

It was my first year and I was trying to survive
As surely as the seniors itching to graduate.

[27]
It was inevitable that he could not stay
For while being the resident radical
Was convenient for those
Who needed to point out
What attitudes or behaviors
Good Catholic students should avoid,

He was not the kind of influence
That donor parents or conservative
Faculty wanted around
Even if he was willing to take
Troublemakers who could not have another
Study hall when Brother Henry needed
To get them somewhere other than his office.

His film class began with 3 and
Ended with 12 who watched and
Then made their own movies.
Funny, inventive, super-8's
That said as much about their lives
As their fascination with classic horror films.

When he was called to the office
Henry made a point of telling
Him what a fine job he had done
With the emphasis on HAD
Before the words,
"Your contract will NOT be renewed"
Left his tongue.

Winona

My world began here
And will end here as well. [28]

We-no-nah
As the train conductor calls from
This stopping place on either side of the river.

Here the pioneers crossed the river ice
Before the first bridge was built;
Here the steamboats moved in cautious
Procession, taking on wood at the bend,
Leaving stumps that measured the progress
Of commerce in the near valleys,
An invitation to be settled farm fields.

We-Know-Now
That each season in time
Is marked with a color, a sound, a name

Beyond the four calendar seasons.
This one the long pain of ice,
That one sudden mud, another rattlesnake heat,
Then blood harvest, all beneath canopy stars
Circling Polaris, twirling as if pulled
By a child's glee, bringing fog's soft cloak
Through the valley.

I see through memory haze
My plunging down the valley walls
On twisted trails of county gravel roads
Or the cracked cement of the old State highway
The curtain of trees torn back

[28]
A summer camp sojourn between
High school and a return to the repeated
Landscape of dreams was a reminder
That he was artist as well as babysitter.

Biding his time until the end
Of July before waving to camper buses
Headed south, and his heading west
Felt like "time served". It was
One and done, no need to repeat.

He would look back at a few pictures,
Have a story or two as evidence.

What he couldn't hold was the smell
Of pines, the sound of the paddle
In moonlight taking him across dark water
To watch cabin lights going out
One after another as the dome of Heaven
Turned to meet the horizon.

What he longed for was another
Geography, also of trees and water,
That he had not realized spoke to him
Beyond college campus, or the town bar.
Elusive and elemental, The Mississippi
Was embedded in emotions and imagination.

To reveal the river and the far bluffs
Then drawn closed with the next turn.

Winona
Where the great river runs west to east
In its long descent from source Itasca to the Gulf.

The steady clock of days
Change ever in motion, unobserved,
As ripening of fruit on the Tree of Knowledge
Before the Fall (whether with snake
Or with simple pride) when we come full faced
With our owned sin before the sweat of our brow,
The seed of our loins, the nakedness that must be covered.

The valley is the bramble bush with a bleating ram
Waiting for Abraham to wet the soil with his quick blade.
Between yesterday's faith and destiny's promise
My somatic brain, sees the distant line of horizon,
Knows what I would sacrifice to stay.   My past
Offered on the altar of could, should, while I dream of return
To the ever changing, never changing river.

Winona
Time warp geography, dream time,
Mythic time, forgotten time

Where the real clock is river time
The rise and fall of waves, deadfalls,
Eddies, the movement of the snapping turtle.
Catfish time, gossamer dragonfly wing time,
Snowy egret time, Canadian goose flyway time,
Thin ice time, cracking ice time, rising flood time
Here in the backwaters.

Say it again
Where Quaking Aspen listen to the moon,
It is Milkweed and Queen Anne's lace time.

Winona
Like a Chinese watercolor, now smoke and fog
A blush of white suggesting something darker.

Oblivion brushed lightly over moss and stone,
The view is eternal, indistinct,
The years interchangeable in the gray embrace
Of rain dappled mornings and cattail soft nights
To wonder which year is this when I descend
Into the waiting valley from Rochester,
Returning once more as a Prodigal Son.

End of the Road

We lived at the end of the road
Where the bus and milk truck turned
Around rather than plunge down
The rutted gravel path
That was the short way to the valley.

We lived in a house at the end of its days. [29]
The insulation, if there ever was any,
Long gone and the single wood
Heating stove in the kitchen unable
To keep more than that room warm.

We lived in the kitchen with the summer
Fly strip hanging from the single electric light.
The table was for eating, for writing,
For reading, for making the model
Of the Universe Gregory worked on all winter.

We lived with the end of money,
The end of work, and for myself the end
Of expectations about tomorrow and
Yet the day after I was thrown out, I thought
I was finally right where I needed to be.

[29]
Gregory had found the place.
He ignored the state of the house
But stood on a stump
Surveying the night sky.

Farmer Johnsgaard lived
Across the road,
Went to bed early,
Turned off the yard lights.

Gregory had the great
Dome of Heaven to himself
And by time he arrived
Gregory had set up
A 6-inch telescope and begun
Photographing every sunrise
And sunset crossing the horizon.

Everything else was beside the point.

Everything else was something
Gregory could put up with
To stand beneath the stars.

Pharmacological Accounting

The first Marijuana: summer of 1967
A thin joint smoked with Billy Shue
On the railroad bridge over the Mississippi
Catty corner from the Brothers' house
On Nicollet Island.

The first Moroccan hashish: summer of 1968.
In a car with the best man driving us
To a bar in Eyota, MN to celebrate
Former Brother John S's wedding.

The first LSD: summer of 1969   [30]
On the Mississippi river in a Latch Island
Boathouse watching a July thunderstorm.
I wondered if God was a 12-barge tow,
Its engine thrum the earth's vibration.

The first mescaline: summer of 1970
At the 4th of July picnic in Trempleau, WI
With Mad Donald before a baseball game
Where us rag-tag mostly tripping "hippies"
Beat the local police department 6 - 4.

The first psilocybin: summer of 1971
At the girls only summer camp
I was teaching at before taking a canoe
On the lake to watch the Pleiades' falling.

The first peyote: summer of 1972
For a ritual at Roger Lacher's place in the Wiscoy
Valley that began with Brother Michael's
Drumming the night and ended with six naked
Men wearing mud skins at dawn.

[30]
Each time a new door was opened
He asked would he be closer to God
Or himself for the experience?

Bad trips?
No, but a couple of
Boring ones where even
The munchies seemed unappealing.

There was that third time he and Doug Wood
Did a tab before eating some bad chili
Big Bertha served at the Happy Chef.
It was hard to tell where the acid left off
And the food poisoning began.
They saw rainbows coming out of every
Orifice as they lay in the bottom of a Latch
Island boathouse praying for a quick death.

Reading a Borrowed Book

The scribble in the margin says,
"Our task is to transform
Human beings, to liberate us
From our own stupidity..."   [31]
And curious as it is, true as it
Might be – what gives me pause

A single sentence highlighted in yellow
- "Memories held too dear
Will devour their host." While
Outside a crow stretches its wings
In the late summer sun, calls out
As if to ask, how dear must

Our memories be to begin the
Self-cannibalizing feast? My
Childhood is imagined like that
Told by cousins and siblings
Of the uncles who let us sip
Homemade wine at supper

Or the aunts who deliberately left
Packs of cigarettes where the curious
Might find them. A past true and not
According to who tells it. I pick up
The pen, add two exclamation points
Next to the accusing margin note.

[31]
He agreed with Fellini
Who said,

"I have
Invented myself entirely:
A childhood,
A personality,
Longings, dreams, and
Memories,
All in order
To enable me
To tell them."

December 1971

Snow in December as a too thin blanket
Hiding, just barely, hardened black dirt
While cornstalks stand broken
        Yet sunny days provide the feeling
        Of a yielding spring
Such a long way off rather than the
Beginning of the real cold.

Gray green grasses, dry milkweed swaying
As a warm wind from the west
Betrays the calendar.

The farm sits at the end of the milk road   [32]
Two icy ruts with mud frozen edges
Bump and buck the few automobiles that appear.
Their destinations – somewhere -- not ours.

As long as we're on the farm it is
        Cut the wood
        Feed the fire
        Keep the pump pulling
        Water from a slumbering earth.

We tell ourselves the house will be
Our warm burrow
        If we keep the fire fed.

Forgetfulness makes it a freezer.

The smoke smell clinging to everything
Greets you at the door
Is a reminder of what must be done.

[32]
Years later it was easy
To romanticize a farm
Without running water
Or indoor toilet,
A wood burning stove,
The fact that they paid
$100 in the summer
And nothing in December
Or January.

Easy after the fact,
But in the during he was
Not so enamored of the daily
Grind when too many
Things needed to be done –
Wood to split,
Fire built,
Water pumped -

Wood by size: logs, scrap, kindling, splinters
In buckets along the wall, we trod
        The little path from entry
        To exit carrying a pail
        Of yesterday's heat
Retracing our steps to the woodpile to
Scatter ashes and
Bring in an armful when we return.

Heavy quilts and sleeping bags in the one room
That has a chance of heat if you leave the door open
While no warmth will reach the couch
        Where I will spend the season.

We learn comfort in layers in the hard months.
        Sweaters – thin for the heated portions
        Thick for everywhere else – are the norm.
Thin and thick socks, gloves, wool hats, wool scarves,
Insulated bib overalls and boots,
Long underwear for the really cold months
Which is every month November to March
Worn as a second skin from shower to shower.

This is the life we have, the world we inhabit.

Just to survive
With the three of them
Needing to do it
Every dammed day.

He would sometimes say,
"I went back to the land and
Failed to take root..."

Sext

Chopping Wood

The wood stove's demand,
The fire's gift in December,
Begins in June the year before
Or so the old farmers said,
Though not so elegantly.

True enough it was, the axe
In hand, we'd split wood
From the sections cut
The length of the stove's
Cast iron fire box.

There is a music in the act,
Swing, steel head fall,
If right, split all the way to the block,
If not, lifted for a second blow
Where the blade is stuck.

Then stacked to the windows
In rows along the side of the house
That gets afternoon sun or
The prevailing winds to dry
Until loosened from winter's grip.

Carried to the mud room,
Restacked to thaw whatever ice
Or mouse having sought refuge,   [33]
Each arriving at the box next
To the stove to serve final duty.

From November to April,
The stove is fed pine and birch,
By day, then banked with the oak
Overnight, in a constant transfiguration
Of ashes from the axe's hard labor.

[33]
He couldn't blame the mouse
In the dresser for wanting to make
A safe nest. He wanted the same
When burrowed in a sleeping bag,
Knowing there will be frost
On the rip-stop in the morning.

He'd hesitate to be the first up
As the first would have to stoke
The stove now gone cold
Or almost. It meant stirring ashes
In search of last embers, then
Coaxing a flame to paper
With careful breath,
Then adding scrap before
A dry split log and only then
Could he make morning coffee.

That hesitancy was not
The mouse's problem,
Since house was freezing every
Winter morning, it was his.
He was the one that disturbed
Mrs. Mouse's rest when he opened
The dresser drawer to pull out
Another pair of wool socks.

Michael H. Makes His Final Vows

Having postponed it all through the summer
He resolved to do the deed at breakfast.

The stove is warm on an October morning
Hissing and crackling wet wood fits and starts.
Michael H. sat down at the bare wooden table
Waiting for the water to boil
And made his solemn final vows. [34]

We talk about the founder, De La Salle
With a nod to his portrait hanging somewhere.

Stirring the oatmeal, Michael says
Now this is poverty, vow or not, living
On $275 a month plus food stamps.

This is our celibacy: three men
In four rooms without lovers though
Sometimes golden boys or dark eyed girls
Arrive and leave satisfied or as satisfied as
One can be using an outhouse.

As to the other vow, the real source of trouble,
We are always obedient to ourselves,
To circumstance, and still be faithful to
The spirit of the Founder's call to serve
Others even on these meager stipends.

[34]
In the Christian Brothers
You took annual vows
For seven years and
By then you knew what
You were in for
And the Brothers
Knew what they could expect
When you petitioned
To make that final pledge.

Afterwards you could leave
If you wanted to
(Many did.
Michael H. did two
Or three years after his final vows.)
But the community could
Not force you out once
Those vows were made.

When he was denied his
Request for final vows
It was not for lack of poverty,

He spooned the steaming oatmeal into a bowl,
Added raw milk, butter, brown sugar.
The vows formally read, picked up the pen
And signed. When oatmeal plopped on the signature,
Michael said, that stain is my witness.

From that day forward he was to be called Happy
Having committed himself to an eternity of joy.

He offered too much of that,
Or failed celibacy or obedience.
The most damming accusation
Was that "the trouble"
Was not what heresy he believed,
But like Martin Luther, he continued
Saying it out loud.

Brother Theodore Visits

(Concerning the visit of Brother Theodore
To the farm community of the New Way School
For the purposes of the reviewing of complaints
About certain matters of religious and District
Policy that do not seem to be practiced
In said community.) [35]

1)
One September evening
Before the simple meal of pork chops and greens
Was over Brother Marty picked
A brownie from the plate and ate it.
Then ate another.
Brother Gregory did not say a word,
Brother Happy did not say a word.

I did not say one either until he had eaten
His third and asked, "what are the crunchy
Things?" Seeds, I believe, seeds and walnuts.
Two brownies later
Brother Theodore watched
Marty fall off his chair laughing
Like he had never laughed before.

2)
No, we did not attend services
Daily or even weekly for that matter
Unless they coincided with a trip
To the college to shower, wash clothes,
Drink the better booze the faculty offered
But we did pray, every day, in earnest
That the truck would start, the stove stay lit.

[35]
What did he believe?
What did he practice?

In those years he would not
Debate how many angels might
Sit on a pin or even
How you would recognize
One if you met them.

He lived in a world where
Fifteen-year-olds were
Looking at six years in
Red Wing for whatever sins
Brought them to court.

 He was asked over
And over again to welcome
The stranger, guide them to
Reclamation with a GED
And some job skills,
Mostly how to show up
On time, ready to work.

That he did not look like
Or live like Brothers in
Suburban schools who

Yes, there were others living
In the house, men, women even, not married
To each other but we could not be sure
Because we did not ask, we simply
Offered the bed and bread to anyone
Who stood at the door needing hospitality -
Even you, Brother Theodore, even you.

Played golf on weekends
Was not an accident.
It was a mechanic's grease
Stained apron.

With Brother S. Charles

Pointing at the bones of something
(A fox perhaps or a large cat)
He said form follows function –   [36]
Look at the length of the leg bone,
The curve of joint, the spine –
The whole bred to hunt,
Long strides, lithe, then swivel, turn...

I could imagine that but not until
I let go of the beauty of the bones themselves
The ankle bone connected to the leg bone,
The leg bone connected to the knee bone,
The knee bone connected to the thigh bone -
Like sculpted alabaster, saying, pick me up
Make a flute that I might howl again

Or a beater upon stretched skin
Replicating my pulsing heart,
My footfall through the forest,
That I may live after living as does
All we eat, one spirit feeding another,
One flesh given over to satisfy another
Whose hunger is unabated.

[36]
He saw the end coming
Not from his choice
But from the circumstance
Of not being able
To disguise what he believed
Any longer.

Years, later, one of his
 Former classmates said,
"If you'd stayed,
You'd have been #1,
The Provincial, by now."

Perhaps, but at what price?

He could not save the Order
From itself by himself.
Those who could were already gone
Or soon would be.

Turning World

Late on afternoon Gregory took me
Out past the barn
        To the point
Where the ridge fell away on each side
Summer corn there,
        The pasture here with cows
        Leaning towards the valley
To watch the sun set.

He said, it is two minutes
Forty-five seconds
        From the moment one edge
        Touches the horizon
To the last bit sinking from view
But
        And this was the point,
But the sun
Does not move, and that disappearing act
Is really the measure of time -
        A metronome,
Our planetary axis
A centrifuge,
No matter how firmly our feet are planted.

Heeding the lesson [37]
I stood facing the rose red horizon,
Felt myself on the turning world
        Falling backwards into night.

[37]
Once he felt
The earth turning
It stayed with him.

The moment you are
Given a wide enough expanse
You can see the curve
Of the horizon,
The ball of globe in motion,
Falling away
Or if you'd rather, pushing
Forward a celestial
Ship on the oscillating seas.

Day and night,
The seasons,
The moon,
All in motion.

His blood, breath,
Even cells pulsing,
While beneath and behind
It all the vibration of atoms
Through the empty
Between of matter as energy,
As consciousness itself
Declaring "I am" and "we are"
Simultaneously.

When Was the Moment?

When I knew I could not stay,
When the prayers would be unanswered,
When I would be unfaithful,

When I fell on my knees in gratitude,
When I put my shoulder to the wheel,
When all doubt was removed, [38]

When the fear was finally named,
When there was no turning back,
When my great heart opened?

[38]
From end to end
He naively believed the work
Of redeeming the world would
Sustain him though the irony
Of it was
After his appeal
Had been rejected
He was living in the same house,
With the same people -
Happy (Michael) was
No longer in the Order,
But Gregory was -
Each doing that same work
For the same poverty wages.

What had he lost?
A title?
Insurance?
The use of the showers
Or a glass of decent
Single malt Scotch at the
College faculty house?

Those he loved,
Those that loved him,
Knew whatever his title
The work remained.

An Unsent Letter

As difficult to write as this is
It is more difficult to live.
        Seven years
(a goodly biblical figure of fullness)
Have given me a chance to
Share with lives and work
Under the name
        Christian Brother.

If thank you is not enough, so it goes.
If my life has been honest,
Then this moment
Was a calculated risk to embrace
        A particular kind of poverty
        Not of spirit but of fact,
        A very personal if not always
        Consistent celibacy,
        Obedience to the spirit
        Of making a better world
        Always informed by choice.
My choice, right or wrong.

Now this community has decided to
        Deny me that life
Within the Society by making my final vows
And while the District Chapter agreed to allow
Those mechanisms of appeal to proceed
        As they should
To Brother Superior, Charles Henry,
        And be rejected.

        Finality is that.

Now I don't think of this as my leaving
The Brothers
As much as a kind of separation of lovers
        (Albeit quarrelsome
As often as not, but lovers still)
With you having sent me into exile
Until you are able to see that
        We are really not so different.

But in truth, we are so different.

There is no negativity, no bitterness   [39]

But rather a moment of hesitation
Before I continue the work
        I am still engaged in.
        I trust you will do the same.

Battersby, in his life of the Founder, says that
"John Baptist De la Salle finally came to the point
Where he had lost everything:
        Money, status, reputation,
        In short, he was free."

And so, I pray that you, my Brothers
Might find in your selves the courage
To risk everything in service to the poor
And the vows, whatever they might mean
        To you who hold them
        And to me, denied the same.

Let us live the values we wish to embody.

[39]
This was a lie,
For the bare truth was that when
He left the Order he was angry
Enough to not speak
To those that rejected him for
Another nine years.

It was only with an Invitation
To come to the 200th
Anniversary of the founding
Of the Christian Brothers
That he saw those who left
Intent on changing the world
But came back for dinner
For the sake of "fraternity"
Outnumbered
Those who stayed.

It was then he realized
Forgiveness was as much
A gift to himself as to
Anyone at the banquet table.

In these years of work in Winona,
In the river bottoms, I have begun to understand
What De La Salle might have intended
        In this working for
        And with the poor.

I regret none of it.

I apologize for nothing for it has been joyous,
Even when it was not obvious
That this suffering would pass
Or this objection to grace would be answered.

        Thank you for the opportunity

If I cannot change the world from within
        Your ranks
I will change it from without,
        For changing the world in the name
Of peace and justice is always the work.

Goodbye and hello again.

None

At 50

Things to learn (or relearn) as I grow older:

1) How to be alone
2) How to be in the moment
3) How to acknowledge being worthy of love
4) How to love without fear
5) The limits of one's body
6) How to reconcile money and principle
7) How to play
8) How to give and receive gifts
9) How to be compassionate
10) The rituals that balance us [40]

[40]
By his 50th birthday,
He had been out of the Order
For 25 years and yet
The entering and leaving remained
The great shadow,
The fulcrum of his being in the world.

There had been two wives,
Several girlfriends in between.
Work of one sort or another
That he took for the puzzle
It offered until he quit
Or got fired once it was determined
The puzzle could or could not be solved

For his 50th birthday,
He bought himself a Jaguar sedan.
It was not a mid-life crisis,
That took another form.
It was a long- distance road car
That let him drive 500 miles a day
And still be sociable upon arrival.

Two Brothers

Two gay men stood
        As my closest companions
        In and out of the Order
        Between ages 18 and 30,
        Though I did not think it
        Significant at the time [41]
        Because it was not
        About the flesh, but
        The possibility of
        Living as if each day
        Were our last.

True though it was
        Both are lost to me now -
        Mad Donald to AIDS
Now as many years ago
From his passing
        As I had known him then,
        And Gregory to dementia such
        That he does not recognize
        Me or even himself
In the stories I tell him
About our lives together.

There is no larger truth
        In this knowing except that we
        Must take whatever grace comes,
        Welcome every messenger
Knocking at the door,
Let them sit in Elijah's vacant seat
For those God has sent
May come in disguise

[41]
Long after Michael P.
Left they talked about
How many Brothers
Were "closeted".

Michael thought 1/3
Which seemed larger
Than he would have guessed
But what did he know?

That was the tragedy
Of the time before
Stonewall and after the
Inquisition, when the
Holy Catholic Church
Held that view the
Beloved Apostle John
Resting his head on Jesus'
Breast was nothing
But a figure of speech.

Grateful for the hearth bread,
	Even if you cannot know
	The gifts they offer
	Until they are gone.

Conversation with a Man Dead
Some Years Now

Sitting in the hospice bed Donald offers chocolates
And I notice that the ones he doesn't like

Have been bitten and placed back in the box.
I eat them though I don't like them either.

We are talking about nothing, because the fact
Of why he is here will not change the outcome. [42]

"Didn't you used to throw dishes out the back
Window to the alley dumpster rather than wash them?"

"They were a nickel apiece at St. Vincent de Paul.
Besides, I only did it on nights we had parties."

"We had parties every week – foreign exchange students,
Bikers, Latch Island hippies, and a few nuns if I remember."

"Yes, I was always surprised when the nuns showed up
But that didn't mean they shouldn't be invited."

He scratches his head, "didn't one of them come asking
For kissing lessons when she was leaving the convent?"

"True enough. She was a fast learner and last I saw of her
She was on the back of Tommy Figs' Harley, heading west."

"When was that?" "At your graduation party though you
Probably were doing a half tab of sunshine at the time."

He wonders what became of Tommy Figs.

[42]
His Generation sang
"I hope I die
Before I get old"
And those who hadn't
Already succumbed to 'Nam
Or the needle,
AIDS or bad luck,
Stood at the edge
Of a supposed retirement
As witness to cancer.
Heart attack, stroke.

He supposed we should
Have seen it coming but
We rode a wave
Of American prosperity and
Digital fancy to comfortable denial.

It seemed to him that
It was past time to wake up,
Ask,
What legacy is worth
Our making?

I wonder if she thought I was a good kisser.

"Not as good as me," he says. "You should try
Changing polarity sometime. It might surprise you."

For the record I did. It didn't. The stubble got in the way
but leaning over his hospital bed, it was my gift to offer.

Variation on an Old Poem

Outside the wind is howling,
Branches sway, leaves depart,
The cold future is late arriving
And hurries, pretending,
It was like this, weeks ago.

I know these gray afternoon skies
Deep in my bones which complain
How many more years   [43]
Of winter are the seedbed of silence,
Repository of heavy coats, scarves, hats

Pulled close? This is not some nameless dread,
This one has familiar nicknames cursed
Through clenched teeth, icy breath.
The wind says, here is my knife,
Remember me, with my quick blade?

.

[43]
There are crows calling
The 4:30 AM watch;
Cats asking to be fed
With an insistent paw on his cheek.

How did his life come to be - get up,
Make coffee, read political blogs
Wait for the newspaper's
6:00 AM arrival?

Is it too much?
A trivialized tick tock
Of life flowing away that says
Why do you sleep?

The hours are precious and few,
His dreams, repetitions of faulty memory.
If only he could reclaim the ones
He had when he was twenty.
Those visions of faith were held high,
Dreamt before he began to count his
Failures and disappointments.

'If only" is the name of death
While we are still in our body.

Those old Zen masters had it right
It is good to be awake.

A Confession

The ones I love are many
And should be so for the fallacy
Of one love like one true religion   [44]

Was never mine. I look at
A picture of two laughing women.
I love both in all their beauty,

In all their bad habits, in all their talents
And generosity. How could I not?
They bring so much joy to the world.

What changes is not the fact
Of my loving someone or some ones
But how the "for" and "with" are manifest.

I might be singular, sequential in
Marriage, plural in single life
But I will not deny myself the joy

Of love for the sake of should,
Ought or regret. As Whitman said,
I contain multitudes. We all do.

[44]
After the 2nd marriage ended, he settled
Into a cream-colored bachelor flat
In a nondescript building, whose sole
Redeeming feature was not the leaky
Ceiling or overly anxious smoke alarm

That rang every time he cooked bacon
But a generous balcony where he could sit
In the cool of night smoking a cigar,
Watching the lights of downtown offices to
The right and Loring Park on the left.

He'd chat politics, philosophy, theology,
Commentaries on the pirouette of cars
Looking for a place to park, art, love
And the reasons they would or wouldn't
Engage in coitus with whoever was visiting.

He was happy with a Weber steps
Beyond the sliding glass, sipping a
Single malt while waiting to turn the steak,
Whatever the circumstance that had brought
Him to this place, it was a gift he cherished.

At LaGuardia

Waiting for a flight I had a Caesar salad and
A dry martini and wept as I actually tasted it,

Or maybe it was my allergies, or the fact
That I am going to die before I'm ready,

Before every last "I love you" or holding close.
No matter that we all face this end. [45]

I am counting the days, saying, "There it is..."
Like that grunt in Tim O'Brien's *The Things
They Carried* telling the newly arrived
"You can't change what won't be changed"

And death is one of those things. Yours, mine,
Ours, the only question worth asking is not

Where or when, but what did I bring to the
World that made this life worth the losing?

Angie the waitress brought me a second vodka
(Off the books) asking me if there was anything
Else she could do to make my day better and I
Replied, "Do you like working in Terminal C?"

She smiled and said her father thinks she's nuts
Serving strangers all day but if food makes us

Happy, why shouldn't she bring that joy? And on
Hearing that I added another five bucks to her tip.

This is what life has become for me, giving away
That which has no value when the curtain falls

[45]
There was a year he was
Going to memorial services
Every month.

When he looked at his
Hands they were
His father's hands before
The Old Man had a 2nd stroke.

No matter that his father
Was 92 when he left this realm,
He, the son, thirty years younger –

Genetics is destiny,
He said to himself as he looked
At his palm
And tried to read his lifeline.

On Buddha's birthday

On Buddha's birthday I wonder
If there should be a celebration?

A rice cake with a little candle, yes,
Or should I sit and let the thought
Of the candle blow itself out?

In the days of sainted Ken Feit, he'd light [46]
A match and sing, "Happy Birthday",
Then blow out the match and sing
Very softly, "Happy death day".

[46]
When he first met Ken Feit in '67
Ken was a Jesuit in Milwaukee,

But when they met again in '72 he had just finished
Ringling Brothers clown school,

And by '80 Ken had claimed the title –
"Holy Fool" – and was happily wandering the world.

Truth be told he was that and we were graced by it.

In '81, an accident ended that blessed fool's tale.

Vespers

This Broken World

This broken world
Has been promised
To the meek.

Who labor
With their hands
As their fathers did.

The truth be told
That same labor
Must always be done. [47]

Let us live this only day
And labor honestly
Without Heaven.

Without Hell
Without reincarnation
In this world.

Make love
Eat bread
Tell jokes.

Give birth
Endure pain
Accept death.

Yes, Heaven
Is another word
I cannot use

[47]
Are you a Tzadikim Nistarim?
Elijah or St. Peter come to supper?
Are you a Bodhisattva?
The Guest met at last?

No none of them.

Are you the Devil?

No again.

He wondered, was it true
That "the poor you shall
Always have with you"?

He wondered, if it was true
The man lost in the forest
Knows all the paths
That do not lead "out"?

Another place
That I do not
Expect to see.

He once heard that a line
Of Sufi's came to a place with two pools,
One was water, the other fire
And those that chose
Water emerged in flames
While those who would burn
Emerged whole again.

Which pool he wondered,
Would he choose?

For Deb on Holy Thursday

I am reminded of the decade
We two made our own Passover   [48]
Broke bread, drank wine,
Saw movies, tenderly held
Each other's secrets, sorrows,
Hands as we walked the river road
Year after year as a ritual nod to
A Church we no longer knew.

This is how you mark the Holy:
You bring yourself to the small
Things and pay attention to
The way your hand fits in another's
Or the taste of warm bread and honey,
The power of Saint Anthony Falls in spring flood,
Or the sound of your breath before
You turn to go back to your life.

[48]
Even after faith is gone
Some rituals remain that
Mark what used to be.

Holy Week was one of his.

Jesus enters Jerusalem
On a donkey, a sly joke
At the expense of Roman
Authority and the next day
Drove the money changers
From the temple.
Neither makes him friends
In high places.

Thursday marks Passover.
The traditional meal is repurposed,
The metaphorical table,
Now models Leonardo's fresco.

It all points to Friday,
With betrayal,
Trial, and death that
He found wanting.
            Not that it wasn't
Necessary for the story
But it seemed to him that the
Church got stuck on the pain,
Not the rolling back of the stone.

For him, the empty tomb
Was the point and
If he had his way
Every Church would take down
The cross in favor of
        An open casket.

Easter Morning

I remember the year we chained ourselves to
The communion rail of the cathedral
To protest the Bishop's support for war.
Easter morning found me
At the grist mill in Pickwick. The water
Still turned the wheel but the grindstone
Rested as the sun chased the cold out
Of the shadowed valley once more.

What matter whether the tomb was empty
I thought, God creates the Garden every day
And I taste of the Tree of Knowing,
I part the Red Sea, wander the desert for forty
Years in search of a Promised Land,
Suffer for somebody's sins on the beam,
Descend into the dark and am re-membered.   [49]
So began life after the Church on my pilgrim path.

[49]
He was familiar with death now.

He understood that
Dying is a mystery
In its completeness.

Fearing loss, the looming grief
We want them to come back;
Cannot understand
Why we did not also go --
How the moment of release
Is theirs completely,
They leave alone
And we are left
To live.

To wait our turn.

Selfies Before Selfies

In most of them I wear sunglasses
(Cool aviator lenses, usually) though the same
Style, they change size from one decade to another

In those years I was a faux Hunter S. Thompson
With my black T-shirt and baseball cap
Before I could afford linen suits and straw hats.

I examine tweeds and herringbones for a hint of the year
As I used to wear the same one till it was worn out
Or when cigars and traveling companions appeared.

The year of Hollis with a constellation of freckles.
The two tours with gap-tooth Sharon performing
"Why Romance is Impossible" (at least between us).

The Indiana of Kris's boyhood before he divorced.
Dorothy & Susan before the ménage-a-trois.
Donald, Diego, Boa and Patrick in Fargo and Detroit.

I always look at what I am driving – the VW
Sirocco of the late '70s through the circus tour,
The red Saab, the blue Jaguar of the Chicago sojourn.

A gray Saab (the one that rolled over on I-35
At 70 mph) and the one after it, before I bought
The Volvo from a poet downsizing expectation.

Whatever car, the selfies were shot from the same angle – [50]
Polaroid camera on the dashboard, me behind the wheel
Driving somewhere, looking happy. And I was most of the time.

[50]
The first wife had given
Him a Polaroid camera
As a parting gift.

It also was the first of many
He collected. In the old days
He left a loaded SX-70 in the Jaguar's
Glove compartment.

When he decided to scan
40 years of images into digital files
He stopped counting after 5,000
With two banker's boxes
Of out of focus pictures
Yet to be examined.

Snowy Monday Morning in Minneapolis

Tom Waits should be singing

      About postcards from hookers
On a day soft and mournful as this.

In fact, he did and radio's playing it
Now can be the Universe having
A laugh or sheer dumb luck.   [51]

This bowl of steel cut oatmeal
With honey offers a meditation on
Why the shovel is happy to be used.

Even if it is only once. When we
Know our purpose says the Buddha

We joyfully do what must be done.

[51]
The Sufi poet, Kabir
(As translated by Robert Bly)
Says:

"Friend, hope for the Guest
While you are alive,
Jump into experience
While you are alive!

Think   and think
While you are alive.
What you call "salvation"
Belongs to the time
        Before Death.

If you don't break your ropes
While you are alive,
        Do you think
        Ghosts
        Will do it after?"

A World of Hurt

Though we have a map
Of that unexplored world,
The diagnosis does us no good.

Back in the day [52]
They used to say
"Any road will do
If you don't know
Where you want to go."

No matter the name of the disease,
The disruption of habit is an invitation
To consider what choice offers.

We know all too well
Where we want to go
But every treatment, every road
That leads to an exit,
Offers a memorial service

While nothing we recognize
Is called
The road to happiness.

[52]
When as a fumbling teen
He practiced (like so many guys did)
Unhooking the bra,
He wanted to be smooth, assured,
But practice never made perfect.

Put to the test in the steamed window
Passion of parked cars
Girls could do it without hesitation,
Under sweaters, with one hand,
But why should they?

And yes, when finally, some generous Miss
Let him touch the Holy Grail, place his
Hand upon that curve of possibility,
A nipple hard with the promise
Of some later ripened fullness,

It did not occur to him that
In years still unconsidered,
She would stand
Naked before cold mirrors,
Her own hands searching for the hidden,
Lumpen omen of loss.

When grade school nuns told him
Our bodies were temples of the Holy Spirit
He did not think to ask
If cancer began with a fugitive touch
Or consider, even for even a moment,
That his fingers were despoiling graffiti.

Hiatus

I had a dream that I was happy
But happy about what was a mystery.

I had a dream that I was well
But when I woke, I was coughing.

That is the way dreams work
They fill in the gaps, make smooth

The rough and unfinished,
The ought to be the day excludes.

In dreams we are transformed
As if they are the blueprint

For what should and will be,
Absolution and forgiveness.

In dreams we take that fork [53]
in the road, not looking back.

Wake up, wake up comes the call
You are not a butterfly, not yet.

[53]
He liked the ambiguity of the reference
To Chinese philosopher
Zhuangzi's Taoist parable of
Not knowing whether
He was a man dreaming he was a butterfly,
Or whether
He was a butterfly, dreaming he was a man.

He came to consider if who
He was now as a measure of whom
He was when the twig was first bent

And the tree followed.

Compline

Ordination Day

(For Charlie Ellis)

There are different gifts
But it is the same spirit that gives them.
There are different ways to serve
But it is the same Grace that is offered.

By the Buddha, by Kali, by Yahweh,
By Zeus, by Thor, by Jesus, by Isis,
By Ra, by any name of any God
You want to offer, all those spoken
Reverent on tongues of fire are lighting a dark
Night until the Universe is ablaze with
The names to confer blessings and
Command us to stand in accepting silence. [54]

Here is the truth we dare not speak:
That it is not I alone but another
Voice that speaks within me.
That it is not I alone but
A community that acts through me
And that it is not the conscious I
But the spirit of the Divine moving the
Waters – no ego, no id – the unknown
And unknowable wholly Other
Who I have embraced as my own.

Paul was on the road and the clouds split
With a peal of thunder, the light blinds
And he did not say, "Oh, I was struck" but
That "I was called" and stumbling to
What he had rejected, embraced the call.

[54]
In cold chapels
He would end the day with
Compline's recitation of
"Now Lord you may dismiss
Your servant,
In peace according to
Your word... "
Which to his mind
Was a small liturgical step from
"And now I lay me down
To Sleep, I pray the Lord
My soul to keep...."
But
Identical in intention.
Seven years of Catholic
Theology, five years of
Philosophy. Two years of
Comparative Religions had
Given him a sense of Christian,
Jewish, Islamic and Buddhist
Traditions. All paid for and
Much of it taught by the Order.

He confessed that in the end
What served his faith was
          Living in the present
With an attitude of gratitude.

We are reeds shaken by the wind
Crying the desert, crying before the dry bones,
Crying with the tablets in hand, crying in the
Valley of the shadow of Death – repent!

Or so they say in that church language you both
Love and hate for its lack of nuance or compassion.

For whatever good it will do any of us. Repent
And turn your hand to the work of creation,
The blessing of the same, and the forgiveness
That must be offered to ourselves most of all.

We were born to die [55]
Yet you remind me, we are alive in the spirit of
Mumble, mumble, something that gives
Life, that frees us to dance to beating drums.

Already dead, you say, our feet move in the dust.
By night we shed the garments that bind.
You say, let us not worry about what we shall eat
Or where we shall sleep – it will be provided.

Already dead, having admitted death is the final clause
Of Life's binding contract, we take another step.
Knowing that, our corpse is witness to love's gifts
And this thing you call the resurrection of Life.

Resurrection comes with every waking,
And as you say, love is the law of life.

So too this affirmation of your priesthood
Which is the laying on of hands and the lifting

[55]
He sometimes believed confession was not
Good for the soul. The truth coming out
Is often not the truth, but a convenient story
That shame told you when you gave it
Permission to marry guilt.

He believed in forgiveness,
Most of all, for yourself, is what mattered.

Nothing can be undone
Except wanting to not be there, then,
To not do or have done whatever.
It there was an Original Sin, it was
Our inability to forgive.

But we are here, now, in this life, still living.

He believed in compassion
And in the nub that it meant we should be kind
To each other as a gift, as a protection,
As our common bond if for no other reason
Then the unarguable fact Death comes for us all.

Up of hearts is a kind of raising up from the dead
That consecrates you in your faith and service.

Holy God, mighty God, wholly God manifest,
As the light comes through you, your fingers
Impart a blessing, the voice sparks conscience.

If you believe...   yes, that's the key,
          If you believe
Then it is not lies or foolishness or the dead weight
Of history but the embrace of possibility, here and now
The dancing promise of love and compassion.

Be that promise in faith and service.

Gregory

You're not dead yet
Or at least not that I have been told.
For the assisted living staff
In Texas actually informing me
That you have departed
Is a matter of chance, dependent on a nurse
On duty reading the file notes.
Taking time to call or send an email
Or a copy of the obituary.

I want you to be alive for selfish reasons.
Just as I want you to be who you
Were before the stroke.
But of course, when I last saw you
That man had already departed
Leaving only the smiling bliss
Of a Zen that was now
Empty of desire and memory. [56]

It was what you always sought
Though for me, seeing you living
Without the knowing what was past,
Who was sitting before you, is heartbreaking -
Still, I sat and told you
Stories of your life in the years we shared.

You liked yourself in some of them
And even remarked on it once,
With a twinkle in your eye as you said it.
For a second the man I knew came
To the surface then slipped away and
I never saw that man again.

[56]
This is the grief before death
That everyone who knows
Dementia or Alzheimer's
Has sat with.
The loved one there yet not there,
You not able to bring
Them back to what matters,
Or what you want to have matter.

He clings to the past,
A past only one of them remembers
Or is the silence deliberate?
Why? He suspects it is not
For their own sake as they
Grow empty of language but
For his, for a space for him to claim
The lost "You"
He wants to hold as
A refutation of emptiness.

The body stilled,
Sent to earth or fire.

The few books on the nursing home
Shelf will be packed or given away.
The pictures of unknown
Persons and places, the clothes
No longer worn
Dispersed or disposed of.

I said thank you and I love you
For who you were,
Who you are, even in this chimera
Guise, fearing you will not understand
Except by the vibration of my hand
On yours and even that declaration
Is too little, too late.

We all become a name
Spoken in the past tense.

He does not need the books.

He needs the stories and
With them – your name still living.

What It's Like

She said to me
Death is a slow
Seemingly inert
Predator
Always just out of view
Even when you know it's close.

Until it's too late and
All that's left
Is the shock of "after" [57]

It reminded me
Of the old Sufi story
Of the Dervish on a boat
In a storm -
Sleeping
As passengers panic.

Finally, the storm passes,
The boat arrives
At harbor.

As he steps on shore
Someone says to him
How remarkable it was
The he remained calm
When there was only a plank
Between them and Death.

He replies,
"Yes, but now
Even the plank is gone."

[57]
When Baba Ram Das
Said "Be here now"
Not even he knew
How difficult it was to "be"
Or what "here" meant,
And certainly not the
Joy and terror of "now".

Those three little words
Are a lifetime of work
To sidestep everything
He was taught to value
- Status, race, religion
Responsibility, obligation,
And yes, Desire.

Most of all the duality of
A comfortable past and
A promising future.

Plague Year

1)
"Surely the rich boarding themselves in their
High walled castles and the monks in the abbeys
Escaped the contagion," said she, "while the poor
Went about the business of dying." [58]

"Not so, for wherever a rat might crawl
Death followed," I said, "though as is always
True, the ragged poor fell like sheaths of wheat
Before the scythe, while those behind the locked
Door met pestilence wearing velvet and lace."

"It is different now, is it not,' said she, "for we
Know whence the infection comes and how
To lift up those who fall."

"Not so, for the rich have not changed and
The poor labor still," I said, "while in the days of
The Black Death there was but one God and one
Infection, today there is a second and it is called
Profit for it puts the golden calf above all else
Though some mistakenly call it Liberty."

2)
In the 132nd day of self-quarantine in the plague year
I find myself pecking at idleness, scratching memory,
Walking one end to another to look out windows
And think: out there the day proceeds without care
As to whether we are here or not and that is as it
Should be for we have spent too many years thinking
That out there was nothing if not for our convenience.

[58]
He often thought about
The effect of the Black Death.
It also originated in Asia,
Arrived in Europe in 1347,
And killed somewhere between
85 and 200 million within five years.

Few knew how it was
Spread but everyone knew
Black boils appeared
In the groin and under
The arms before the fever.

In some villages
100% of the population perished,
Crows disposed of the corpses.

Beside the funeral pyres
Children sang:
"Ring around the roses,
A pocket full of posies,
Ashes, ashes,
We all fall down..."

In the 132nd day of alone I revert to remembering
The sweetness of a kiss, the feel of skin in an embrace

As if I were reading the history of a lost civilization
Wondering if that empire will rise again, even if it is
The last thing we ever do in this necessary isolation.

Whoever said hope is a bird with wings has not   [59]
Studied beak and claw. The world prepares for after.
Turkeys already cross against the light, the deer
Nibble the lawn. Soon bears will sleep in
500 count sheets and raid the fridge as we once did.

59
Yes, he said, this is a gloss
On Emily Dickinson's
 "Hope is
The thing with feathers
That perches in the soul –
And sings the tune
Without the words-
And never stops – at all – "

It was not that he disliked
Her sentiment but rather
That reality is not necessarily
Comforting.

"Once" is the Way it Begins

Sometimes 'Once upon a time" but that designation
Of "time" is unnecessary. "Once" designates.

Not now. Then. Whenever what follows was.
In some time - usually past
But it could just as easily be a future.
There is a moment recounted.   [60]

Once we ate fresh anchovies, sliced and grilled, served
With good crusted bread, soft cheese and wine.
Maybe a chilled Pinot Grigio or sharp Retsina
But more likely a full-bodied red.
Table wine on a white tablecloth.
The smell of the sea called to mind though not seen.

Once, crossing Iowa after a missed turn,
Large barns passed in the blink of an eye.
A red-tailed hawk swooped up, rode the current,
Lifted over the windshield
Without damaging either of us.
It was an omen. Rightly so.

Once she came to my bed, early in the morning.
Unexpected but appreciated, pressed her hips to mine
As we spooned. Took my hardness in stride.
Held my hand in hers against the curve of her belly.
Deflected a kiss.
When it was time for breakfast, she returned to her room
And to the mystery of why.

Once the old barber cutting my hair had a heart attack.
A half-done crew cut. The clippers gouged

[60]
He was looking at old files,
Yellowed letters
Received and brittle carbons
Of ones he sent and
Marveled that so many of the themes
He writes about now,
He wrote about then.

Had he learned nothing
Or did he see the future
And place channel markers
In filing cabinets and banker boxes
To guide himself
Through his yet to be
Charted history?

As he dropped to the floor.
The buzz there beside my ear. Gone.
Skidding, a slithering snake on the floor
Before they fell silent.
He was dead. I needed a new barber.

Once a monk. Once faithful. Once an apostate. Once a husband.
Once a father. Once a lover. Once a thief. Once a martyr.
Once a magician. Once a child. Once dead. Once called to life.

Once there were dragons. Giants. Witches. Kings.
Wolves and bears, though they are still with us they are not the same.

In "once" the world is more intense, more slippery.
Fraught with all manner of challenges, dangers,
The mechanisms of magic and reward.
The archetypes of who we are or could become.

Enter once and do what can or must be done.
Exit once and life goes on.
What glass? half full or half empty now?
What changed? You? The world?

All these once and a billion others that are
Both ordinary life and not.
Called to mind, to attention, they are invitations for more.

Crow Wisdom

On an afternoon sunlit path
A crow stands calling my attention
The way they do when the world
As I know it is about to be turned
          Upside down. [61]

Then
I remember the story about the rabbi
Who in times of trouble,
Goes to a certain place in the forest,
Says a certain prayer, performs
          A certain ritual,
And the trouble passes.

The next rabbi knows
The place and the prayer
          But not the ritual,
The rabbi after him knows
The prayer but not the place
And the one after him
Knows nothing – not the place,
          Not the ritual,
Not the prayer, only the entering
Of the forest and the story
Of those who proceeded him
          But that is enough.

Another step and the air is filled
With crows lifting off bare branches,
Swooping in trios and quartets
Their shadows marking the path
          Before me

[61]
At his age
He knew that
Should, would, could
Count for little.
What counts for much
Is be and do.

Waking up has become
The miracle of the day –
Alive, yes, still alive
And in possession
Of some sense of self
And purpose.

Even the slow
Shallow water coursing
Along the riverbed
Will wear away stone
In the long drift to the sea.

He'd have to look at
Those old maps to see
How flood and drought
Have changed that course
And to old photos
To trace the first appearance
Of polished stones
Just beneath the surface.

Like emergency lights
In the smoke-filled plane
After the landing gear
Collapsed, the doors flung open.

People complained
That they had to leave laptops
Or take off their high heels to slide
Down the yellow chutes.

What don't you understand?

This very moment
Requires us to at least and at last
                Make an effort...

Whether
Airplane, election or love affair,
                Panic ensues.

The crows call out instructions:
                This is that time,
This is that place,
                Forget any rituals
Say the God dammed prayer
                And jump!

Even when it is not visible
Be and do continues
As he wades
Into the water with a sieve
Looking for gold.

He says to himself
It is the looking that counts,
Not the finding.

That Day Comes Again

Year after year grief presides
Over the feast of memory, offering
Thin sour soup and spilled milk.

The calendar does not care nor lie,
So don't look at it.
Not looking will not change what was. [62]

Here, the field. There the forest.
This is the only photograph you kept
To remind you how long the path.

Birth and death with whatever is in between,
A few short hours of happiness
As place markers on a map of tears.

[62]
In that moment
He remembered singing
The Compline verses in the cold
Chapel on a Sunday night:

"Be sober, watchful and vigilant!
For your adversary,
The devil, as a roaring lion,
Goes about seeking
Someone to devour.
Resist him…"

Even then he knew
That the adversary's name
Was not the devil,
But the self,
And whether one could
Make peace with yourself
Was what these many years later
He still prayed for.

About the Author

Loren Niemi began storytelling as a child fibber but soon decided that he was less interested in telling lies than in improving the truth.

He is an innovative storyteller, creating, coaching, directing, performing, producing, teaching and writing about stories that matter for audiences of all ages in urban and rural settings for over forty years. He has participated in over 200 poetry and story slams since 1995 and has won seventy-three first, second, or third places and two grand slams, as well as being a member of the Minnesota team for the 1998 National Poetry Slam.

He has also done thirty-three Fringe Festivals in eight cities as solo or ensemble storytelling performances since 1996. Howard Lieberman has been his performing partner for seventeen of them, proving as Paul Burchill said in the *LA Times*: "These two are fascinating performers who manage to whip up a theatrical experience from little more than their mouths and imaginations."

Loren published *What Haunts Us*, a collection of non-traditional ghost stories, which won a 2020 Midwest Book Award for "Sci-Fi/ Horror /Fantasy / Paranormal" fiction. Other publications include two poetry chapbooks, *Coyote Flies Coach* and *Vote Coyote!* and the award-winning *The New Book of Plots* and its companion *Point of View and the Emotional Arc of Stories,* which he co-authored with Nancy Donoval and focused on the structuring of oral and written narratives.

He also co-authored with Elizabeth Ellis the critically acclaimed, *Inviting the Wolf In: Thinking About Difficult Stories* on the value and neccessity of stories that are hard to hear and harder to tell. Not being afraid of those unnerving stories has been one of the hallmarks of his performances.

Loren has an MA in Liberal Studies with a focus on American Culture from Hamline University (St. Paul) and a double BA in Philosophy and Studio Arts from St. Mary's University (Winona). He is a 2016 recipient of the National Storytelling Network's Lifetime Achievement Award.

For more informationo: www.lorenNiemistories.com

Made in the USA
Middletown, DE
30 July 2022